START-UP
ART AND DESIGN

SELF-PORTRAIT

Louise and Richard Spilsbury

Evans

Published by Evans Brothers Limited
2A Portman Mansions
Chiltern Street
London W1U 6NR

Produced for Evans Brothers Limited by
White-Thomson Publishing Ltd.
Bridgewater Business Centre, 210 High Street,
Lewes, East Sussex BN7 2NH

Printed in China by WKT Co. Ltd.

Editor: Rachel Minay
Consultant: Susan Ogier Horwood, Art Education
Consultant specialising in Early Years and
Primary age range
Designer: Leishman Design

British Library Cataloguing in Publication Data
Spilsbury, Louise
    Self-Portrait. – (Start-Up Art and Design)
    1. Self-portraits - Juvenile literature
    I. Title II. Spilsbury, Richard, 1963-
    704.9'42

ISBN-13: 9780237533960

Acknowledgements:
Special thanks to Ms J. Arundell and pupils at Mayfield
Primary School, Hanwell, West London, for their help
and involvement in the preparation of this book.

Picture Acknowledgements:
Bridgeman Art Library pp. 4l (Giraudon), 8, 14r
(Giraudon); Corbis pp. 4r (Francis G. Mayer), 5l (ROB
& SAS), 5r (image100), 13 (Gianni Dagli Orti); Chris
Fairclough pp. cover tr & main, title page, 6, 7, 10, 11l,
12t, 17l, 18l, 19tl, 20t&b, 21; iStockphoto.com pp. cover
tl, 16 (all).

Artwork:
Pupils at Mayfield Primary School, Hanwell, West
London pp. 9r, 12b (all), 18r, 17r; Tabitha Halliday, age
6, pp. 11r, 15; Emelia Halliday, age 7, p. 14l; Rachel
Minay pp. 19tr, 19bl&r; Robert Sheppard, age 7, p. 9l.

Contents

What is a self-portrait?

Self-portraits are pictures people make of themselves. Self-portraits can tell us what artists look like, or about their lives or feelings.

What do these self-portraits tell you about the artists?

self-portraits   artists

What is special about you? How would you show yourself in a self-portrait?

"I would paint a picture of me with my grandmother. She looks like me."

"I would do a self-portrait of me playing football with my best friend."

special

Pencil self-portraits

Some self-portraits show only the artist's face.

▲ Compare your face with a friend's.
What is different and what is the same?

compare   shading   tones

Shading **is when you use one colour to make light and dark** tones.

► **Look in a** mirror. **Where are the dark and light areas on your face?**

"Part of my face is in shadow."

light

slightly dark

very dark

◄ **How hard must you press a pencil to draw shades like this?**

mirror   shadow

Planning a portrait

◄ **Queen Elizabeth I always dressed up for her portrait. She wore jewels and expensive clothes to show she was rich and powerful.**

What will you wear in your self-portrait? What does the style you choose say about you?

portrait style

What **props** will you include? Artists show their **identity** in the objects or people they put in their self-portraits.

What do these self-portraits tell us?

props   **identity**

Paint effects

Clare's class uses brushes and other objects to create different textures with paint.

"I'm using a comb to show the texture of my hair."

textures   experiment

▼ The children experiment with colours. They mix paints to make a skin tone that closely matches their own. What colours would you mix to make your skin tone?

Tip: Look after your equipment. Wash brushes and pack paints away afterwards.

▲ Tabitha mixed paint to match her skin tone, then added her features with other media. What do you think she used?

features   media

Mood pictures

▶ Chandra's class reads *'The Owl who was Afraid of the Dark'*. The children discuss fear and other emotions.

▼ What emotions do these mood pictures show?

emotions   mood

► This artist used colour and swirling paint textures to express his mood. Does his facial expression tell you how he is feeling?

▼ Chandra's class thinks of colours to suggest different moods.

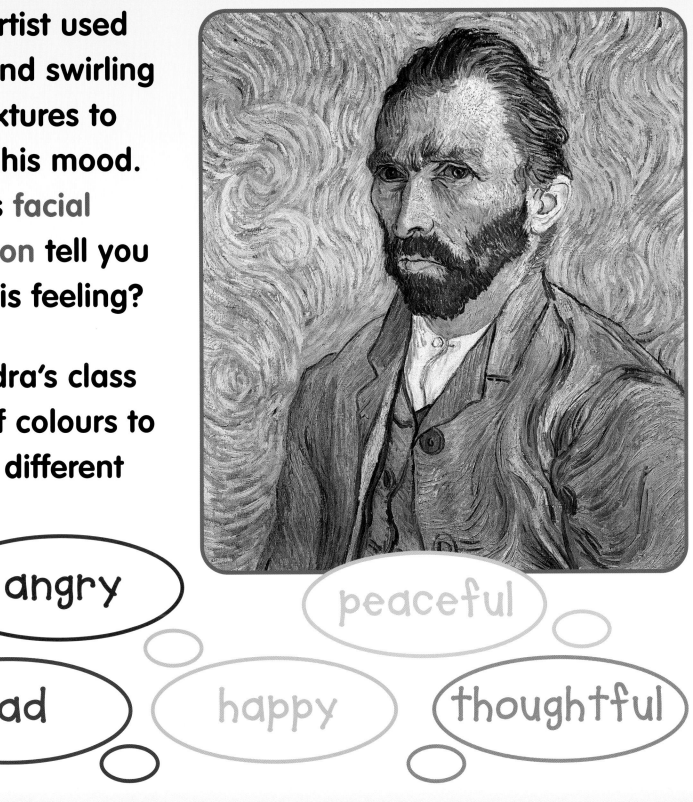

angry

peaceful

sad

happy

thoughtful

facial expression

Symbolic art

► This portrait of a **pharaoh** includes **symbols** with special meanings. The eye ... **represents** perfection.

◄ Emelia drew herself in **profile**. How else is her picture similar to the pharaoh's?

pharaoh symbols represents

Some self-portraits don't show people at all. They use symbols to show the artist's personality.

◄ Draw around your hand and colour it in. Fill the spaces with images that say something about you.

Life-size collage

A **collage** is made by sticking paper and other **materials** on to a flat surface. Maya's class draws **outlines** of each other to make **life-size** self-portraits.

Match these adjectives to the materials Maya collected.

furry shiny smooth bumpy soft silky

collage   materials   outlines

The children rip paper and cut **fabric** to make different-sized pieces for their collage.

"I plaited this wool to make soft hair."

Photo faces

Amir's class takes digital photos of each other. They try different **poses** and **gestures**.

▶ **Sasha made an alter ego self-portrait with her photo. Which sides of her personality does it show?**

poses   gestures   alter ego

▼ **Amir uses an effects tool on the computer to create an unusual self-portrait.**

► **Some children use the computer to overlap lots of different photos. This kind of picture is called a** photomontage**.**

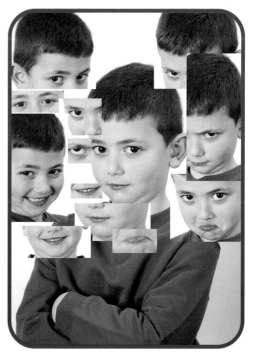

photomontage

19

On display

▲ **What do you think** frames **do to a picture?**

◀ **You could make a colourful frame for your self-portrait. Think about** symmetry **in your design.**

frames   symmetry

The children **review** their work. They think about what they would **improve** or do differently in future.

review   improve

Further information for

New words listed in the text:

adjectives	fabric	improve	personality	represents	symbols
alter ego	facial expression	life-size	pharaoh	review	symmetry
artists	features	materials	photomontage	self-portraits	textures
collage	frames	media	portrait	shading	tones
compare	gestures	mirror	poses	shadow	
emotions	identity	mood	profile	special	
experiment	images	outlines	props	style	

Possible Activities

PAGES 4-5

The first self-portrait on page 4 is *Myself, Portrait-Landscape* (1890) by Henri Rousseau. It shows him about to retire from his job as a customs officer and take his place as an artist in Paris. The second image, *Self-portrait with Daughter* (1789) by Élisabeth-Louise Vigée-Le Brun, is much more personal and intimate.

The children could collect family portraits and spot resemblances (link with Science Unit 2C, Variation). Then they could draw how they think they will look when they are adults! They could also draw self-portraits that include family members.

PAGES 6-7

To help the children look more closely you could play a game. One child leaves the room and the others have to describe her or him from memory. Tell me about the way X looks. Can you remember what clothes Y was wearing?

Do a drag and drop activity to draw a portrait online at http://www.mrpicassohead.com/create.html

Children could try drawing pencil portraits without taking the pencil off the paper, or by drawing with their eyes shut, or by drawing with one hand what the other feels as they run their fingers over their face.

PAGES 8-9

Local museums and galleries may do workshops or talks linked to self-portraits. Or you can download information from the National Portrait Gallery (http://www.npg.org.uk/live/edelearning.asp) and adapt it to visit your local gallery. Children could research and be inspired by many different artists. A self-portrait inspired by Georges Seurat and pointillism could use cotton buds to make dots to fill in hair, skin and clothes. Or children could do a cubist self-portrait inspired by a Picasso.

PAGES 10-11

Children could enlarge their pencil self-portraits on the photocopier and then try out different effects on the copies. They could mix glue and paint and experiment with this and different brushes to create surface patterns and textures.

Parents and Teachers

PAGES 12-13

Children could research the Arcimboldo portraits made using fruit and flowers to show the parts of the face and draw a face of their own using different objects for parts of the face. The class could explore Picasso's fawn plates. The children could draw self-portraits on paper plates, perhaps even choosing an animal's face to represent them.

PAGES 14-15

Children could do a symbolic self-portrait using images that represent something about them. For example, if they are interested in cooking, they could make a collage with pasta and pictures of food from magazines cut into the shapes of their features.

PAGES 16-17

At http://www.article19.com/shockwave/makeaface.htm there is a drop and drag activity for children to create faces with different moods.

Children could also make clay faces by pressing fingers and tools into the surface of clay, and building up a 3D texture. They could create a number of faces expressing a range of different emotions.

Children could experiment with colour using their photocopied line portraits (see notes for pages 10–11). They can try colouring the copies to see how different colours can change a picture's mood. They could also use coloured gels or transparencies to change the colours instantly.

PAGES 18-19

After taking a digital photo, use the effect tools in a program such as Paint Shop Pro to make a line or charcoal drawing of the photo. This can be used as an aid to assist with children's portrait drawing. ArtRage is an art package for your computer

Further Information

BOOKS FOR CHILDREN
What Is a Self-Portrait? (Art's Alive!) by Ruth Thompson (Sea to Sea Publications, 2005)

I'm Good at Art (Read & Learn) by Eileen Day (Raintree, 2004)

Line and Tone (How Artists Use...) by Paul Flux (Heinemann Library, 2007)

Pattern and Texture (How Artists Use...) by Paul Flux (Heinemann Library, 2007)

WEBSITES
http://www.fm.coe.uh.edu/resources/portrait_detectives/pd_criteria.html
http://www.drawingpower.org.uk
http://www.tate.org.uk/learning/kids

that is free to download.

Children could research the photomontages of David Hockney and use these as inspiration for their own photomontages.

PAGES 20-21

Frames in galleries celebrate and emphasise artists' paintings and pictures. When children frame their pictures, they could give them a title and date them, too.

A class could arrange a self-portrait competition, either in a gallery or by uploading photos of the class portraits on to the school website. The children could ask parents to match each child's name to his or her self-portrait.

Index